ANIMALS ON THE BRINK

Giant Pandas

Karen Dudley

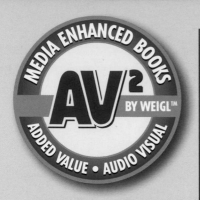

AV² provides enriched content that supplements and complements this book. Weigl's AV² books strive to create inspired learning and engage young minds in a total learning experience.

Your AV² Media Enhanced books come alive with...

Audio
Listen to sections of the book read aloud.

Key Words
Study vocabulary, and complete a matching word activity.

Video
Watch informative video clips.

Quizzes
Test your knowledge.

Go to **www.av2books.com**, and enter this book's unique code.

BOOK CODE

K 7 7 3 8 4 4

Embedded Weblinks
Gain additional information for research.

Slide Show
View images and captions, and prepare a presentation.

AV² by Weigl brings you media enhanced books that support active learning.

Try This!
Complete activities and hands-on experiments.

... and much, much more!

Published by AV² by Weigl
350 5ᵗʰ Avenue, 59ᵗʰ Floor
New York, NY 10118
Website: www.av2books.com   www.weigl.com

Library of Congress Cataloguing in Publication data available upon request.
Fax 1-866-449-3445 for the attention of the Publishing Records department.

ISBN 978-1-61913-433-1 (hard cover)
ISBN 978-1-61913-434-8 (soft cover)

Printed in the United States of America in North Mankato, Minnesota
1 2 3 4 5 6 7 8 9 16 15 14 13 12

052012
WEP170512

Project Coordinator Aaron Carr
Design Mandy Christiansen

Every reasonable effort has been made to trace ownership and to obtain permission to reprint copyright material. The publishers would be pleased to have any errors or omissions brought to their attention so that they may be corrected in subsequent printings.

Photo Credits
Weigl acknowledges Getty Images as its primary photo supplier for this title.

Contents

Take a Stand
Debate · Research

How to take a stand on an issue **5**

Should people try to save the giant panda? **15**

Should giant pandas be kept in captivity? **25**

Should logging and farming be banned where pandas live, despite people's dependence on that land? **31**

The Giant Panda

Giant pandas are often described as cute, cuddly, and lovable. The giant panda's short, flat nose, rounded ears, chubby body, and seemingly enormous eyes have made it a favorite animal for many people around the world. Yet, giant pandas are also creatures that have developed a unique way of surviving in the natural world.

In this book, you will find out what giant pandas eat. You will learn how giant pandas can communicate using scent, even without seeing one another. You will find out as well how they use unique sounds to express a range of emotions. You will discover how mother pandas and their tiny cubs survive in their wet mountain **habitat**. You will also learn what scientists and others are doing to save the panda's habitat and protect this **endangered** animal.

Although young pandas like to stay near their mother, adult pandas are solitary and tend to stay away from each other.

Giant pandas appear to be gentle, but they are very powerful animals.

How to Take a Stand on an Issue

Research is important to the study of any scientific field. When scientists choose a subject to study, they must conduct research to ensure they have a thorough understanding of the topic. They ask questions about the subject and then search for answers. Sometimes, however, there is no clear answer to a question. In these cases, scientists must use the information they have to form a hypothesis, or theory. They must take a stand on one side of an issue or the other. Follow the process below for each Take a Stand section in this book to determine where you stand on these issues.

1. **What Is the Issue?**
   a. Determine a research subject, and form a general question about the subject.

2. **Form a Hypothesis**
   a. Search at the library and online for sources of information on the subject.
   b. Conduct basic research on the subject to narrow down the general question.
   c. Form a hypothesis on the subject based on research to this point.
   d. Make predictions based on the hypothesis. What are the expected results?

3. **Research the Issue**
   a. Conduct extensive research using a variety of sources, including books, scientific journals, and reliable websites.
   b. Collect data on the issue and take notes on all information gathered from research.
   c. Draw conclusions based on the information collected.

4. **Conclusion**
   a. Explain the research findings.
   b. Was the hypothesis proved or disproved?

A Peek at Pandas

Under its fur, the skin of a giant panda is black where its fur is black and pink where its fur is white.

The giant panda's heavy body and slow walk make it seem clumsy at times, but pandas are surprisingly good climbers.

Features

G iant pandas are large **mammals** with many special adaptations that help them survive in their forested mountain habitat. They have thick, waterproof fur to keep them warm and long, sharp claws to climb trees. Giant pandas have strong cheek muscles and huge teeth that are perfect for chewing tough vegetation.

An adult giant panda weighs about 200 to 300 pounds (90 to 135 kilograms). On all fours, it stands about 3 feet (0.9 meters) tall at the shoulder and measures about 5 feet (1.5 m) in length. Males are about 10 percent larger than females.

The giant panda's body shape is well adapted to its forest environment. Strong front legs and heavy, powerful shoulders make giant pandas excellent climbers. Pandas are also flexible, which allows them to move easily through dense bamboo. Their short legs make them very slow walkers. Even when a giant panda is in danger, the fastest it can move is a slow, clumsy-looking trot.

Although a giant panda's fur looks soft and silky, it is actually quite thick and wiry. The hair of an adult giant panda can grow up to 4 inches (10 centimeters) in length. Each hair is coated with an oily substance that keeps the panda's fur dry in its chilly, wet habitat.

The black-and-white markings of giant pandas are unique among mammals. Their ears, shoulders, legs, and eyespots are black. The rest of their fur is creamy white. Scientists have several theories about why the giant panda has such unusual markings. Some **biologists** believe the panda's colors are useful for **camouflage**. In the bamboo forests where pandas live, patterns of light and shadow can make it difficult to see the giant panda's black-and-white markings. Some scientists, however, think that the giant panda's colors are more useful for winter camouflage when snow covers the ground.

Not all scientists believe the giant panda's unusual coloring serves as camouflage. Some think the black-and-white fur helps the animal keep a steady body temperature. While the black fur absorbs heat from sunlight and warms the panda, the white fur reflects sunlight and keeps it cool. Yet another theory is that the giant panda's markings help it avoid other pandas. Like many creatures, giant pandas will threaten another animal by staring at it. The giant panda's large, black eyespots make its eyes look much bigger, so its stare appears to be more aggressive.

Classification

There is only one **species** of giant panda. Scientists have given this species the Latin name *Ailuropoda melanoleuca*. Today, giant pandas live in nature only in small pockets of land in southwestern China.

For years, scientists debated how to classify this unique mammal. Many scientists noticed that giant pandas look a great deal like bears. They have similar brains, ear bones, and respiratory systems. They walk in the same way as bears and, like bears, give birth to tiny cubs. Other scientists claimed that giant pandas were more similar to red pandas, which were once thought to be closely related to raccoons. Unlike some bears, red pandas and giant pandas do not **hibernate**. A giant panda's teeth and skull, and the color pattern of its fur, resemble those of the red panda. Giant pandas and red pandas eat the same foods and live in the same kind of habitat.

Scientists finally conducted genetic testing. This is testing that examines an animal's **genes** to learn more about its origin and its relationship to other animals. Since then, most of the world's scientists have come to agree that giant pandas belong to the bear **family**. Scientists give this family the Latin name *Ursidae*.

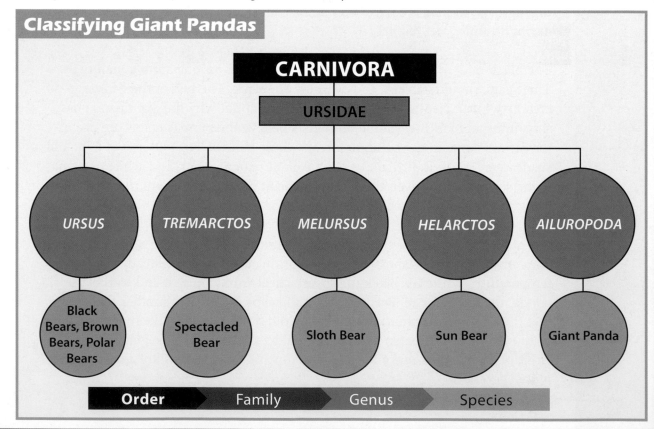

Classifying Giant Pandas

CARNIVORA

URSIDAE

| URSUS | TREMARCTOS | MELURSUS | HELARCTOS | AILUROPODA |
| Black Bears, Brown Bears, Polar Bears | Spectacled Bear | Sloth Bear | Sun Bear | Giant Panda |

Order → Family → Genus → Species

The giant panda's scientific name, *Ailuropoda melanoleuca*, means "black-and-white catfoot." The name comes in part from the red panda, which was sometimes called a firecat.

The red panda, which has the scientific name *Ailurus fulgens*, lives in the cool bamboo forests of China, Myanmar, and Nepal. It shares some of its habitat with the giant panda.

The sun bear, or *Helarctos malayanus*, is the world's smallest bear. It is found in many parts of Southeast Asia, including Myanmar, Laos, Cambodia, Vietnam, Thailand, and Malaysia.

Special Adaptations

Giant pandas eat mostly bamboo, which is a sturdy kind of grass. Thick stalks of bamboo are very difficult to eat, but giant pandas have developed features that are specially adapted for their diet.

Jaw

The giant panda's jaw is very heavy and strong. Its jaw works together with its cheek muscles to break up and chew bamboo stalks. A giant panda's jaw and cheek muscles are so powerful that a panda could easily chew an aluminum dish into tiny pieces.

Teeth

Giant pandas have 42 teeth. Most of their teeth are wide and flat with ridges, and they are well adapted for crushing and chewing. Like humans, giant pandas get two sets of teeth in their lifetime. The giant panda has a much larger skull and teeth than the brown bear, although both animals eat mainly plants. The panda's large teeth have adapted to help the animal eat tough stalks of bamboo.

Face

When you look at the round face of a giant panda, you might think that it looks a little chubby. In fact, the giant panda's face is not fat but gets its shape from very large cheek muscles. These extremely strong muscles help pandas chew their bamboo diet.

Paws

Giant pandas have five fingers and toes with long, sharp claws that allow them to climb trees easily. Their front paws have another special feature. The giant panda has a special "thumb" that sticks out from its palm. This thumb is actually a wrist bone that has grown and developed into a useful tool. It is opposable, which means it sits opposite to the rest of the panda's fingers and can be pinched up against them. A panda can grasp a bamboo stalk by wrapping its fingers around the stalk and squeezing its thumb in to secure its hold.

A Peek at Pandas

Some people think that a giant panda balancing on its front paws to leave a scent mark looks like a gymnast doing a handstand.

Even pandas in captivity will leave scent marks in the area where they live.

Communication

Giant pandas use body language to communicate when they are face-to-face with other pandas. Since pandas avoid direct contact as much as possible, they more commonly use other ways of communicating. Giant pandas communicate by using a combination of different vocal calls and by leaving **scent marks**.

Like human fingerprints, each panda's odor is different from every other panda's odor. Pandas rub the glands on their hindquarters against something to leave an oily liquid as their mark. Pandas can tell the age of another panda and whether it is male or female by its scent mark. They can also tell how long ago the panda made the mark. If a female panda left the mark, other pandas can even tell if she is ready to mate.

There are a variety of ways for a panda to leave its scent mark. Sometimes a panda squats on its hind legs and rubs its hindquarters on a stump or log. A panda may also back against a tree or large rock, balance on its front paws, and lean its back legs against the surface as it marks. Other times, the panda lifts its leg and rubs its hindquarters against an object.

From an Expert

George Schaller is a world-renowned giant panda biologist. Working out of the Wolong Natural Reserve in China, he was part of a team that conducted an important study on giant pandas.

"Years have passed since I last saw giant pandas in the wild, yet their powerful image continues to impinge on my life. Pandas are creatures so gentle and self-contained that they still affect me by the force of their uniqueness, by their aura of mystery." - George Schaller

Body Language

Unlike humans, giant pandas do not make faces to show their moods. Neither do they raise the fur on their bodies or move their ears to communicate fear or aggression, as many other mammals do. Instead, giant pandas communicate by holding their bodies in certain ways. Pandas also use their ability to make different sounds to communicate with one another.

Aggression

When a giant panda wants to threaten another panda or show its superior strength and status, it lowers its head so that its eyespots and ears are visible. Sometimes it will even bob its head up and down or swat at the other panda with its front paws.

Submission

A submissive or weaker panda turns its head to avoid eye contact. It may drop its head completely and cover its eyespots with its paws. The submissive panda may even roll on its back.

Vocalization

Giant pandas can make 12 distinct calling sounds. They combine these sounds in complex combinations that vary in loudness. Each sound has a certain meaning. Sounds are mixed to communicate the panda's mood. A growl or roar communicates aggression or a threat. A huff, snort, chomp, or honk gets across anxiety or worry. Moans barks, yips, and squeals mean the panda is excited. A bleat communicates friendliness.

Distress

A young panda in distress makes a squawking sound. Other animals, such as weasels and leopards, are known to hunt young pandas for food. A mother panda will come running to her cub whenever she hears its distress call. A young panda may also make this sound if it is hungry or lonely. A baby panda prefers to be close to its mother at all times.

Take a Stand
Debate · Research

Should people try to save the giant panda?

Some scientists believe strong action should be taken to protect giant pandas. Others think the giant panda is a remnant species. This means the giant panda is probably becoming **extinct** naturally, not just because of human activity.

FOR

1. Some scientists think the giant panda's problems are directly caused by humans. They believe that if the panda's declining numbers are the result of human activity, then people should do everything possible to save these animals.
2. When people protect the panda's habitat, they also help other endangered animals and plants in the same area.

AGAINST

1. If the giant panda is a remnant species, then efforts to save the panda are interfering with natural processes.
2. Pandas are extremely expensive to take care of. People have spent millions of dollars trying to save them, both in nature and in captivity. Some experts wonder if this money would be better spent protecting a variety of other animals in danger.

A Peek at Pandas

Giant panda mothers are 900 times heavier than their newborn cubs. If this size difference occurred in humans, an 8-pound (3.6-kg) human baby would have a mother that weighed 7,200 pounds (3,250 kg).

Most female giant pandas are able to become pregnant only for a few days to a week every spring. As a result, a relatively small number of giant panda cubs are born each year.

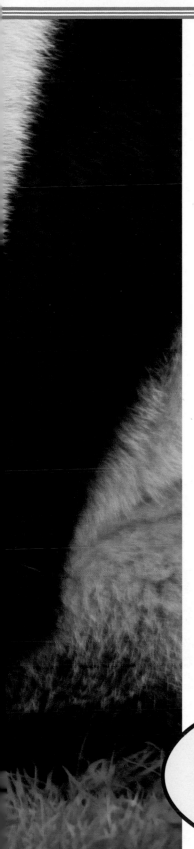

Mating and Birth

The mating season for giant pandas takes place from mid-March to mid-May. During these months, giant pandas spend much of their time looking for mates. They leave scent marks on stumps and logs and call out more often. Their loud calls will often echo throughout the forest.

Female scent marks and vocal calls, such as moans, bleats, and barks, may attract as many as four or five males at a time. The male pandas will often fight each other for the chance to mate with the female. The female may climb up a tree to avoid the conflict.

The entire mating process takes only about two or three days. Apart from the time a cub spends with its mother, this is the only time that giant pandas socialize with other giant pandas. Once they have mated, female and male giant pandas go their separate ways.

The **gestation period** for giant pandas can vary from 97 to 163 days. The reason for this variation is a process called **delayed implantation**. After the mother giant panda becomes pregnant, the cub does not start to grow right away. The cub will start growing only if the mother panda is able to get enough food. Once the cub begins to develop, it will be born about 45 to 60 days later. A giant panda usually gives birth to a single cub. Sometimes twins are born. When this happens, the mother often ignores the weaker cub. She does not have enough energy to care for two cubs.

From an Expert

"(Saving giant pandas means) much more than just dollars and cents. They touch our spirit in a much more fundamental way—hence their ability to evoke such wonder and awe."
- Don Reid

Don Reid is a biologist and leading giant panda expert. He has studied the pandas of the Wolong Natural Reserve with George Schaller and Chinese panda expert Hu Jinchu.

Cubs

Giant panda cubs are usually born in August or September, when bamboo is most abundant. The mother needs a good food supply to stay strong enough to look after her cub. A few days before giving birth, she searches for a good place to make a den. Dens are built close to good sources of food and water. The den must also keep the panda and her cub warm and dry. Giant pandas like to build dens in the hollow stumps of large evergreen trees. They may also build a den in a dense patch of bamboo or in a large crack in a rock.

Giant panda mothers are well known for the care they give to their young. As soon as a mother panda's cub is born, she picks it up and holds it close to her body to keep it warm. She nurses her cub and keeps it clean.

For the first month, the cub stays tucked under her chin, snuggled beneath her arm, or cradled in one of her front paws. When the mother needs to go out of the den to find food, she picks up her cub and carries it gently in her mouth. A mother giant panda sleeps sitting up, with her cub held carefully in her arms.

Although giant panda cubs are very small, they have extremely loud voices. Whenever a young panda is either uncomfortable or hungry, it squawks noisily. The mother responds immediately to her cub's cries. Even though giant pandas are usually very easygoing, a mother panda can be vicious if her cub is in danger.

A female giant panda may raise only five to eight cubs successfully in her lifetime.

A Peek at Pandas

To make her den more comfortable, a mother giant panda lines it with twigs, wood chips, and even young trees.

A new baby panda spends its days sleeping and nursing.

The eyespots of a giant panda cub start out as circles. As the cub grows, the eyespots become shaped like a teardrop.

Development

A giant panda cub is helpless in its first month or so of life. A newborn panda is tiny, pink-skinned, blind, and toothless. It is completely dependent on its mother for food, warmth, and protection. Its eyes are closed, and it is unable to crawl. Newborn giant pandas weigh only 2 to 5 ounces (56 to 140 grams) and measure about 6 inches (15 cm) in length. After a week, the giant panda cub starts to grow its black-and-white fur.

After the first six weeks, a giant panda cub opens its eyes. Its fur is much thicker, and it is able to leave the den with its mother. The giant panda cub grows quickly, but it is still dependent on its mother. She must carry it wherever she goes.

As the young cub continues to grow, it learns how to stand and walk on its short legs. At the age of about 5 months, it begins to eat bamboo. It still drinks its mother's milk, however. By 6 months, the cub weighs about 22 pounds (10 kg.)

At the age of about 8 months, the young giant panda stops nursing and concentrates on eating bamboo. By then, it is able to walk and climb by itself. In the following months, the giant panda learns how to survive in its environment and communicate with other pandas. After one year, a cub weighs about 45 pounds (20 kg). Some cubs leave their mothers when they are about 18 months old, while others stay until they are 24 or 30 months old. Giant pandas are not ready to mate until they are 5 or 6 years old.

Giant panda cubs are good tree climbers and will sometimes climb trees to avoid danger.

Habitat

Giant pandas are not well adapted to live in most habitats. In nature, pandas live only in the Chinese provinces of Sichuan, Gansu, and Shaanxi. Within these provinces, the pandas live in forests high in the mountains.

Giant panda territories must have a great deal of bamboo for the animals to eat, thick bushes for shelter, and large, hollow fir tree trunks for building dens. In searching for food, giant pandas often move up and down the mountain slopes of their habitat. This is because different types of bamboo grow in different areas on the mountain slopes. It is also very important for giant pandas to have a good source of drinking water nearby. If water is far away, the pandas use too much energy trying to get a drink of water.

Organizing the Forest

Earth is home to millions of different **organisms**, all of which have specific survival needs. These organisms rely on their environment, or the place where they live, for their survival. All plants and animals have relationships with their environment. They interact with the environment itself, as well as the other plants and animals within the environment. These interactions create **ecosystems**.

Ecosystems can be broken down into levels of organization. These levels range from a single plant or animal to many species of plants and animals living together in an area.

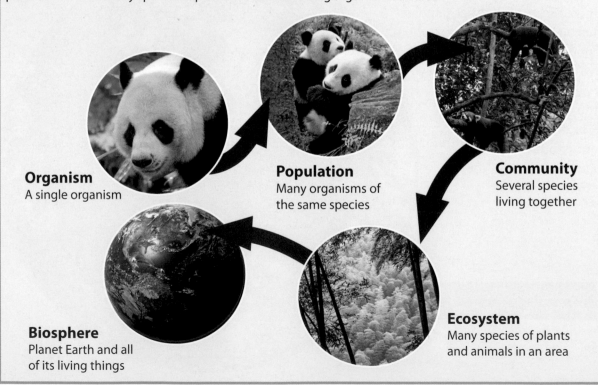

Organism
A single organism

Population
Many organisms of the same species

Community
Several species living together

Biosphere
Planet Earth and all of its living things

Ecosystem
Many species of plants and animals in an area

In its habitat, a panda will ignore an otherwise ideal area if the only water source is more than 0.5 miles (0.8 km) away.

Finding Giant Pandas

Even biologists who study giant pandas have trouble finding them. Giant pandas like to live where bamboo is abundant. Due to their body shape, they can crawl or push their way through the dense growth. Humans often get stuck in bamboo when trying to track pandas.

To study giant pandas, biologists often must first capture them. Biologists set traps that are baited with food. When the giant pandas go after the bait, the trapdoor closes. The biologists then give the panda a tranquilizer. This is a powerful drug that puts the panda to sleep.

Scientists may carry a panda out of the dense bamboo forest to study the animal for a short time.

Once the giant panda is asleep, biologists can examine it. They also often attach a radio collar to the panda's neck. The giant panda slowly wakes from the tranquilizer and is released back into the forest. The collar sends out signals that biologists use to track the panda. This process is called radio tracking, and it is one of the main methods biologists use to learn about pandas in their natural habitat.

Take a Stand
Debate · Research

Should giant pandas be kept in captivity?

The number of giant pandas living in nature is going down because of habitat loss. Giant pandas survive outside of their natural habitat in several zoos and breeding facilities around the world.

FOR

1. Studies of giant pandas in nature are hard to conduct. Pandas live in remote areas that make it difficult for biologists to carry out research. Much of what we know about panda behavior comes from studying captive pandas.
2. In what are called captive breeding programs, scientists try to get pandas to mate and produce cubs in captivity. If captive breeding programs are successful, the giant panda species can be preserved in zoos. A small number of pandas born in captivity are also being released into their natural habitat.

AGAINST

1. Studies of captive giant panda behavior may not be very helpful in understanding pandas living in nature. Captive pandas living in zoos may behave very differently from pandas in their natural habitat.
2. The success rate for breeding pandas in captivity remains fairly low. Giant pandas mate more easily and successfully in nature.

Range

Pandas spend most of their time searching for food in their **home range**. If bamboo is easily available, pandas travel as little as possible. In one month, they may visit only 10 percent of their range. The size of a giant panda's home range depends mostly on how much bamboo grows in the area.

Each female giant panda has her own home range. Within this range, a female usually has a favorite area where she spends most of her time. This area, called a core range, may be as small as 100 acres (40.5 hectares) in size. The core range is centered around the best bamboo patches in a territory. While a female might allow another female into her home range, she will not allow another female into this favorite core area. Sometimes, a male giant panda may share the same home range as a female.

The home range of a male giant panda may overlap the ranges of several females and border the ranges of other males. Unlike female pandas, males do not have a favorite part of their home range. They spend much of their time traveling throughout their entire range. When males meet other males during their travels, they rarely try to defend their territory by attacking and seriously harming each other. They are usually more concerned with establishing their rank. A higher-ranked male panda has a better chance of mating than a lower-ranked panda. Male giant pandas determine their social rank by comparing their size and strength with other males. In these wrestling matches, weaker pandas give way to larger, stronger pandas.

In the winter, a panda will roam its range in search of bamboo stems. While plentiful, stems are not as nutritious as the leaves and shoots that grow in warmer months.

A **Peek** at **Pandas**

Bamboo is an evergreen, which means it stays green even during the colder months. That allows pandas to find and eat bamboo in their range throughout the year.

The home range of male giant pandas is usually larger than that of female pandas.

Diet

In a typical day, a giant panda usually eats for eight hours, sleeps for four hours, and then gets up to start eating again. Ninety-nine percent of what it eats is bamboo. Bamboo stems can grow for many years and become quite woody and tall. About 25 different kinds of bamboo grow in the mountains where pandas live. Pandas especially like to eat umbrella bamboo, arrow bamboo, and golden bamboo.

In the spring, giant pandas eat the nutritious and tender bamboo shoots. These shoots are a good source of **nutrient** protein. During the rest of the year, giant pandas eat bamboo leaves and stalks. On average, a giant panda eats 25 to 30 pounds (11 to 14 kg) of bamboo in one day. During the spring, though, a panda may eat 100 pounds (45 kg) of bamboo shoots in a day. Pandas usually eat the bamboo sitting or lying down. They grasp the shoot or stalk in their forepaws and use their teeth to strip off the tough outer layer to get at the softer fibers inside.

Sometimes, giant pandas will eat other vegetation, such as horsetails, rushes, parsnips, willow leaves, and the bark from fir trees. They will even eat bamboo rats or other animals if they can either catch or scavenge them. Giant pandas like meat, which is very high in protein and other nutrients. They cannot get meat very often, though, because they are not very good hunters. Most of the meat they do eat is carrion. This is an animal that has died of natural causes or has been killed by another animal.

The giant panda's throat has a special lining to protect it from bamboo splinters.

A **Peek** at **Pandas**

Giant pandas have a very good sense of smell. Even at night, they can find the best bamboo stalks by scent.

Eating while sitting allows a giant panda to use all four paws to grasp bamboo stalks.

The Food Cycle

A food cycle shows how energy in the form of food is passed from one living thing to another. As giant pandas feed and move through the bamboo forest, they affect the lives of the animals around them. The feeding habits of the pandas produce changes in the environment. In the diagram below, the arrows show the flow of energy from one living thing to another through a **food web**.

Secondary Consumers
Very rarely, a **predator** such as a leopard, will catch and eat a young or very old giant panda.

Parasites
Pandas provide a home for parasites such as the roundworm.

Primary Consumers
Giant pandas eat bamboo and almost nothing else. They consume bamboo at all stages of its growth. Their strong teeth and jaws rip through thick bamboo stalks, as well as tender shoots and flowers.

Producers
Bamboo plants produce food energy from the Sun. Giant pandas get food energy from eating bamboo. Parts of the bamboo that a panda does not digest become panda droppings that in turn nourish the soil so that new plants can grow.

Decomposers
When giant pandas die, decomposers break down the panda's body materials, adding nutrients to the soil.

Omnivores
Although almost all of their diet is bamboo, giant pandas will sometimes eat small animals, such as pikas or bamboo rats. Sometimes, they also feed on carrion.

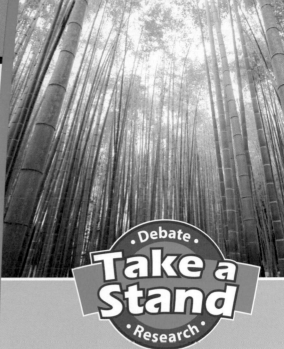

Take a Stand
Debate · Research

Should logging and farming be banned where pandas live, despite people's dependence on that land?

To help protect giant pandas, the Chinese government has outlawed logging and restricted farming in the panda's habitat.

FOR
1. The restoration of bamboo forests in the giant panda's habitat has increased the populations of these and other endangered animals.
2. The regrowth of forests helps prevent the kind of floods that have killed thousands of people in the area. New trees soak up excess rainwater during times of heavy rainfall.

AGAINST
1. Restoring the giant panda's habitat has cost many local Chinese people their livelihoods. In the past, loggers cut down and sold trees from the forest to earn money for their families. Growing crops is another important source of income.
2. Although tourists are visiting the restored panda habitat, this tourist industry has created a relatively small number of jobs.

A **Peek** at **Pandas**

Humans may be the giant panda's biggest competitor, but people are no match when it comes to biting power. Pandas can easily bite through a thick bamboo stalk. Humans would have trouble cutting the same stalk with an ax.

Male panda cubs will often practice their wrestling skills by play fighting.

Competition

Giant pandas lead a solitary existence with one main purpose, which is getting enough food. This focus in a panda's life rarely puts it in conflict or competition with any other animals, including other pandas.

Bamboo is normally so plentiful that there is no need for giant pandas to fight over food. Giant pandas also do not fight for territory. Their system of communication works well enough that they are usually able to avoid one another. Scent marks and other signs let intruders know that another giant panda has claimed an area. In this way, fights over territory that could use up a great deal of energy are easily avoided.

The only time giant pandas may compete with one another is during the mating season. If more than one male wants to mate with a female, the males must decide which one is higher-ranked. Sometimes, these competitions can become aggressive, and two males will wrestle, push, and bite.

The giant panda's most serious competitors are humans. As human populations have grown, human activity has steadily spread in the mountainous areas of China where giant pandas live. Some forests have been cut down so that the wood can be sold or burned as fuel. Other forests have been cleared for agriculture. Many pockets of bamboo forest are now surrounded by open, cultivated land.

With the destruction of their natural habitat, giant pandas are crowding into increasingly smaller areas. Often these pockets of forest have only one species of bamboo. When all the bamboo in an area flowers and dies, giant pandas try to **migrate** to other areas to find different kinds of bamboo that are still growing. If two bamboo forests are separated by farms or villages, the giant pandas cannot migrate and may die of starvation. This is also a problem during the mating season. If a female cannot find a male that she likes in her own territory, she often cannot cross over to a different territory to find a mate. Then, one less panda cub is born.

Cabbage is one of the crops commonly grown by farmers who clear land in areas where the giant panda lives.

Giant Pandas with Other Animals

Aside from the giant panda, only two other animals depend on bamboo for survival. These are red pandas and bamboo rats. Pandas generally avoid or ignore other animals in their environment. It takes a great deal of energy to compete for food, and giant pandas cannot afford to use up that energy.

There are times, however, when finding enough bamboo can be a problem. Most grasses follow a yearly cycle of growth, flowering, and seeding, but bamboo cycles can last 30 to 120 years. When a type of bamboo in an area reaches its flowering cycle, all the bamboo plants flower, put out seeds, and die at the same time. This is called bamboo dieback. In the past, giant pandas and other animals in an area of dieback were able to migrate to another area that had a different kind of bamboo. Today, giant pandas, red pandas, and bamboo rats have lost so much of their habitat to farms and other human activities that it is much more difficult for them to travel to another food source.

An adult giant panda is so large that it does not have many natural enemies. Weasels, martens, wild dogs, and leopards live in China's bamboo forests. All of these predators will attack giant panda cubs. This is one of the reasons why a mother panda keeps such a close watch on her cub. Sometimes, wild dogs or a leopard will prey on an adult panda that is old or sick.

Human hunters are known to catch giant pandas for their valuable pelts. Many of these panda **poachers** believe it is worth the risk to illegally hunt the animals. One giant panda pelt can be sold for as much money as a rural farmer could make in 10 years.

The yellow-throated marten, a powerful animal that can weigh more than 12 pounds (5 kg), has been known to hunt giant panda cubs.

A **Peek** at **Pandas**

The giant panda's digestive system is designed for eating meat. A long time ago, giant pandas were **carnivores** and hunted other animals. At some point in time, they switched over to eating bamboo.

A poacher caught trying to sell a giant panda pelt in China may face a long prison term. Pelts taken from poachers are studied by scientists to learn more about pandas.

Folklore

Folklore, myths, and legends reflect the feelings cultures have about people, animals, and the world they live in. Giant pandas were first mentioned in Chinese writings about 1,200 years ago. Back then, the large, furry bears were rare and treasured possessions of emperors and other people of great importance. It is a bit surprising, therefore, that pandas do not appear very often in Chinese folklore. This may be because giant pandas are shy creatures and difficult to find.

Although giant pandas are not in many Chinese folktales, they do appear in a Tibetan myth. The myth gives an explanation for how giant pandas got their black markings. At the beginning of the story, four young female shepherds are killed when they try to save a panda from a hungry leopard. When the other pandas hear what has happened, they decide to hold a funeral to honor the girls' sacrifice. At this time, according to the myth, giant pandas were pure white, without a single black marking. To honor the dead girls, the pandas arrived at the funeral wearing black armbands. The pandas were so sad that they began to cry. As their tears rolled down, the dye from the armbands began to mix with their tears. The black dye marked the areas where the giant pandas touched themselves and hugged each other. Although the pandas kept these black marks as a reminder of the girls, they also wanted their children to remember what happened. The pandas turned the four shepherds into a mountain with four peaks. According to the myth, this mountain stands in the Sichuan province of China, near the Wolong Natural Reserve.

A computer-animated panda was the star of the popular film *Kung Fu Panda* in 2008. The movie *Kung Fu Panda II* came out in 2011.

Myth	Fact
 Like many bears, giant pandas hibernate during the winter.	Giant pandas do not hibernate. Most bears build up fat in their bodies from all the food they eat in the warmer months, and they live off this fat during the winter. A panda's bamboo diet does not allow it to build up enough fat to hibernate.
 Pandas are cuddly and friendly animals that enjoy being around people.	Pandas are extremely cautious around people and other animals, including other pandas. They prefer to be alone and will avoid contact with others as much as possible. They may climb up a tree if they think another animal is a danger to them.
 Pandas are gentle and will never fight other animals.	Although giant pandas usually avoid conflict, male pandas will fight each other to establish rank. Female pandas can also become quite threatening if a predator tries to attack her cub.

Beloved in China, the giant panda was one of the official mascots for the 2008 Olympic Games held in Beijing, China's capital city.

Status

Fossil evidence shows that giant pandas once lived throughout China. They are now found only in a few small areas. Climate changes caused the bamboo to die off in the lower lands. When this happened, the pandas moved into mountainous regions where bamboo still grew. Ancient climate changes explain why giant panda populations have shrunk in the past. At the present time, however, it is likely that human activities are mostly to blame for the decline of the species.

In the mid-1970s, many giant pandas died of starvation because of a widespread bamboo dieback. Suddenly, people realized that they knew very little about these rare animals, and they began to ask questions. How do giant pandas live? Why did they starve during the dieback? How many giant pandas are left?

These questions prompted extensive studies on the giant panda, as well as a count of the giant panda population. This count took three years to complete, from 1985 to 1988. When the results were in, it was obvious that giant pandas were in serious trouble. Only about 1,000 pandas lived in nature. An additional 100 pandas lived in zoos and other places of captivity.

Around the same time, bamboo on the Qionglai Mountains began flowering and dying. China organized a huge rescue effort to save the pandas from starvation. News of the giant panda crisis reached the rest of the world. Soon, money began to pour in. The crisis turned out to be far less serious than the one in the mid-1970s. Only a few pandas died of starvation. Yet, it helped bring to light the problems that giant pandas were facing.

Since then, scientists and conservation experts have worked to protect and restore the giant panda population. Change has happened slowly. Another count of giant pandas took place in 2004. As a result, scientists believe at least 1,600 pandas exist in nature, with another 300 living in captivity. These numbers are slightly higher than the count in the 1980s.

A Peek at Pandas

Giant pandas are very shy, and their forested habitat is very thick. One biologist who was looking for pandas on a daily basis saw a panda only about once a month, even though 18 giant pandas lived in the area.

One reason that panda populations do not increase quickly even in protected areas is that female pandas almost always give birth to and raise just one cub at a time.

Saving the Giant Panda

In 1984, the U.S. Fish and Wildlife Service listed the giant panda as an endangered species. The international community soon followed. American journalist Nancy Nash, known in China as "Miss Panda," brought the Chinese government and World Wildlife Fund (WWF) together to form a plan to save the giant panda. The WWF is a major international conservation organization. By 1989, China and the WWF had created a conservation plan for giant pandas. The plan's goals included maintaining a population of giant pandas in their natural habitat and restoring that habitat. It also encouraged the breeding of pandas in captivity. The study of giant pandas was another important part of the plan.

Since then, the Chinese government has successfully expanded some of its protected bamboo forests. It has banned logging in protected areas and tried to create safe passageways so pandas can travel between isolated forests. The government also tries to protect giant pandas from poachers. Under Chinese law, a person caught hunting a giant panda may be sentenced to more than 10 years in prison.

By the 2000s, the Chinese government had created more than 50 protected areas for pandas. Those areas cover more than 3.8 million acres (1.5 million ha) of forest. Scientists in China have also begun sending pandas born in captivity into natural habitats. The hope is that those pandas will breed with other pandas to increase the population. Yet, the giant panda remains endangered, and its fate is still uncertain.

As the WWF's international symbol, the panda logo is familiar to people throughout the world.

Distribution of Giant Pandas in China

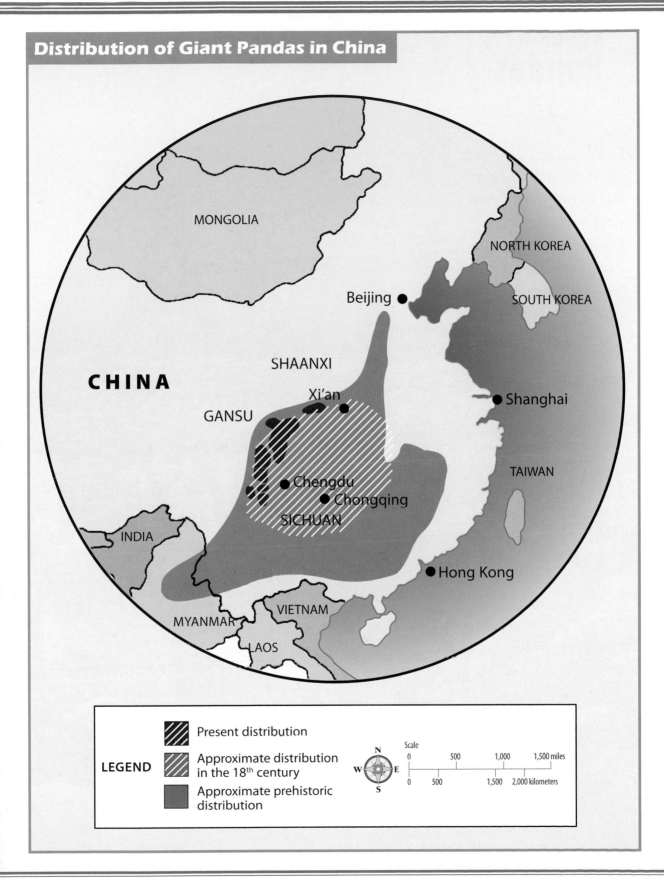

MONGOLIA

NORTH KOREA

SOUTH KOREA

Beijing ●

SHAANXI

CHINA

GANSU

Xi'an ●

● Shanghai

Chengdu ●

● Chongqing

SICHUAN

TAIWAN

INDIA

● Hong Kong

VIETNAM

MYANMAR

LAOS

LEGEND

Present distribution

Approximate distribution in the 18th century

Approximate prehistoric distribution

Scale

0   500   1,000   1,500 miles

0   500   1,500   2,000 kilometers

N
W   E
S

A **Peek** at **Pandas**

Pandas became a beloved part of popular culture in the 1930s, when they were first brought to zoos outside China. Since then, pandas have appeared on everything from mugs and shower curtains to stamps and earmuffs.

In 2008, the WWF displayed 1,600 papier-mâché giant pandas in Paris, France, to symbolize that only about 1,600 of these animals exist in their natural habitat.

Conservation Symbol

Giant pandas have become a worldwide symbol for the need to preserve the variety of life on Earth. The panda's role as symbol has become known worldwide through the work of the WWF. This organization was formed in 1961 when a group of scientists, business people, and government leaders created an organization that would raise money for nature conservation.

The WWF based its work in Switzerland, near the scientific research-based conservation organization known as the International Union for Conservation of Nature and Natural Resources (IUCN). Both groups agreed upon a common mission. They would "harness public opinion and educate the world about the necessity for conservation."

Meanwhile, a giant panda named Chi-Chi had arrived at the London Zoo. At the time, Chi-Chi was the only giant panda in the Western world. Record numbers of people visited the zoo to see the furry black-and-white animal. Knowing they needed a recognizable symbol that would be popular around the world, the WWF founders agreed that the giant panda would be an excellent choice. As the WWF adapted the panda into its logo, the animal began its career as a worldwide conservation symbol.

From an Expert

"Although the giant panda lives only in China, in a very real sense it belongs to the whole world. If we can allow a creature as loved and cherished as the giant panda to vanish from the face of the Earth, what hope is there for the rest of the natural world?" – Keith and Liz Laidler

Keith and Liz Laidler are zoologists and wildlife filmmakers. They are active in wildlife conservation efforts, and they have produced a film, *Pandas of the Sleeping Dragon*, about the giant pandas on the Wolong Natural Reserve.

Back from the Brink

Giant pandas are at risk wherever they live in nature. They are endangered due to habitat destruction and poaching. Just 1,600 or so giant pandas are left in their natural habit, and several hundred more live in captivity. With the efforts of conservationists, giant pandas have regained some of their lost habitat in the mountains of China. Yet, most conservationists believe more work must be done to expand these restored panda reserves and promote an increase in the still-struggling giant panda population.

Giant pandas have survived against great odds, but they still need support from organizations that try to save them, such as the WWF. The WWF not only works to protect giant pandas in their natural environment. It also trains biologists and develops plans and projects to study giant pandas. We still do not know enough about giant pandas. By learning more, we can make better decisions about how to help them.

For more information about the WWF's giant panda rescue program, contact:

World Wildlife Fund
1250 24th Street, N.W. 20037-1193
P.O. Box 97180
Washington, DC 20090-7180

The World Wildlife Fund was the first international conservation organization to be invited by the Chinese government to help it save the giant panda.

Activity

Debating helps people think about ideas thoughtfully and carefully. When people debate, two sides take a different viewpoint on a subject. Each side takes turns presenting arguments to support its view.

Use the Take a Stand sections found throughout this book as a starting point for debate topics. Organize your friends or classmates into two teams. One team will argue in favor of the topic, and the other will argue against. Each team should research the issue thoroughly using reliable sources of information, including books, scientific journals, and trustworthy websites. Take notes of important facts that support your side of the debate. Prepare your argument using these facts to support your opinion.

During the debate, the members of each team are given a set amount of time to make their arguments. The team arguing the For side goes first. They have five minutes to present their case. All members of the team should participate equally. Then, the team arguing the Against side presents its arguments. Each team should take notes of the main points the other team argues.

After both teams have made their arguments, they get three minutes to prepare their **rebuttals**. Teams review their notes from the previous round. The teams focus on trying to disprove each of the main points made by the other team using solid facts. Each team gets three minutes to make its rebuttal. The team arguing the Against side goes first. Students and teachers watching the debate serve as judges. They should try to judge the debate fairly using a standard score sheet, such as the example below.

Criteria	Rate: 1-10	Sample Comments
1. Were the arguments well organized?	8	logical arguments, easy to follow
2. Did team members participate equally?	9	divided time evenly between members
3. Did team members speak loudly and clearly?	3	some members were difficult to hear
4. Were rebuttals specific to the other team's arguments?	6	rebuttals were specific, more facts needed
5. Was respect shown for the other team?	10	all members showed respect to the other team

Quiz

1. In which country do giant pandas live in nature?

2. Do pandas hibernate in the winter?

3. How much does an adult male panda weigh?

4. How do pandas mark their territory?

5. What does a panda cub do when it is distressed?

6. Where does a mother giant panda live with her cub?

7. What food makes up 99 percent of a panda's diet?

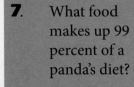

9. How many pandas currently live in nature?

10. What organization features a panda on its logo?

8. What is the panda's biggest competitor?

Key Words

biologists: scientists who study living things

camouflage: when an animal's appearance blends in with its environment so that it is very difficult to see

carnivores: animals that eat other animals

delayed implantation: a process by which an unborn animal does not begin to grow right away in its mother's womb

ecosystems: communities of living things and resources

endangered: a type of plant or animal that exists in such small numbers that it is in danger of no longer surviving in the world

extinct: no longer surviving in the world

family: one of eight major ranks used to classify animals, between order and genus

food web: connecting food chains that show how energy flows from one organism to another through diet

fossil: bone or other remains or evidence of animals that lived very long ago

genes: the building blocks for making a living thing

gestation period: the length of time that a female is pregnant

habitat: the place where an animal lives, grows, and raises its young

hibernate: to pass winter inactively

home range: the entire area in which a giant panda lives

mammals: warm-blooded animals that have hair or fur and nurse their young

migrate: to move from one area to another

nutrient: a substance in food that animals need to live, grow, and be active

organisms: forms of life

poachers: people who kill an animal illegally

predator: an animal that lives by killing other animals for food

rebuttals: attempts to counter, or disprove, an argument

scent marks: the odors a panda leaves behind by rubbing itself on a stump or log

species: groups of individuals with common characteristics

Index

Log on to www.av2books.com

AV² by Weigl brings you media enhanced books that support active learning. Go to www.av2books.com, and enter the special code found on page 2 of this book. You will gain access to enriched and enhanced content that supplements and complements this book. Content includes video, audio, weblinks, quizzes, a slide show, and activities.

Audio
Listen to sections of the book read aloud.

Video
Watch informative video clips.

Embedded Weblinks
Gain additional information for research.

Try This!
Complete activities and hands-on experiments.

WHAT'S ONLINE?

Try This!	Embedded Weblinks	Video	EXTRA FEATURES
Chart the levels of organization within the biosphere.	Learn more about giant pandas.	Watch a video about giant pandas.	**Audio** Listen to sections of the book read aloud.
Map giant panda habitats around the world.	Read about giant panda conservation efforts.	See a giant panda in its natural habitat.	**Key Words** Study vocabulary, and complete a matching word activity.
Complete a food web for giant pandas.	Find out more about giant panda habitats.		
Label and describe the parts of the giant panda.	Discover more fascinating facts about giant pandas.		**Slide Show** View images and captions, and prepare a presentation.
Classify giant pandas using a classification diagram.	Learn more about what you can do to help save giant pandas.		**Quizzes** Test your knowledge.

AV² was built to bridge the gap between print and digital. We encourage you to tell us what you like and what you want to see in the future.

Sign up to be an AV² Ambassador at www.av2books.com/ambassador.